12·50

HEINEMANN CHILDREN'S REFERENCE
a division of Heinemann Educational Books Ltd
Halley Court, Jordan Hill, Oxford OX2 8EJ

OXFORD LONDON EDINBURGH
MELBOURNE SYDNEY AUCKLAND
MADRID ATHENS BOLOGNA
SINGAPORE IBADAN NAIROBI HARARE
GABORONE KINGSTON PORTSMOUTH NH(USA)

ISBN 0 431 00308 4

British Library Cataloguing in Publication Data
Bailey, Donna
    Swimming.
    1. Swimming – For Children
    I.   Title   II.   Series
    797.2'1

Editorial consultant: Donna Bailey
Designed by Richard Garratt Design
Picture research by Jennifer Garratt

Photographs:
Cover: Lupe Cunha Photo Library
Allsport: 21, 22, 23, 24
Peter Greenland: title page, 2, 3, 4, 5, 6, 7, 8, 9, 10, 11, 12, 13,
    14, 15, 16, 17
Hutchison Library: 32 (Hilly Janes), 31
Mary Rose Trust: 28
Tony Stone Worldwide: 19 (Thomas Zimmermann), 26
    (Chris Harvey), 27 (Mike Smith), 30 (Paul Berger), 18, 20,
    25, 29

Printed in Hong Kong

90 91 92 93 94 95 10 9 8 7 6 5 4 3 2 1

Swimming

Donna Bailey

HEINEMANN

I'm going to swim in the big pool
for the first time today.

2

My teacher puts some armbands on me.
These will help keep me afloat.

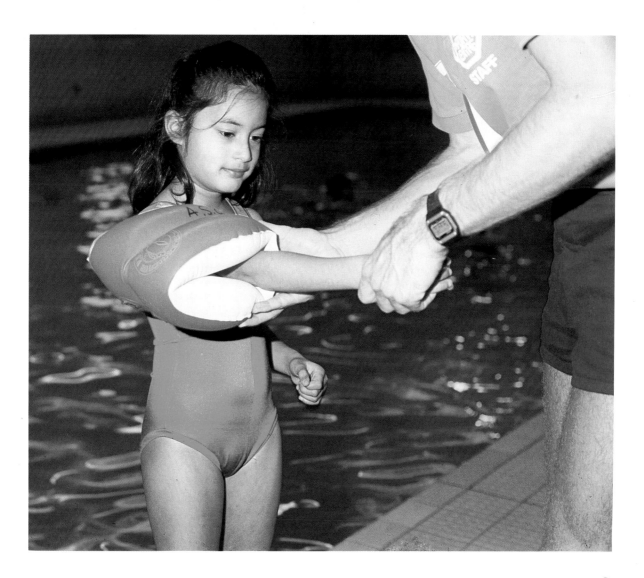

I get in the shallow end.
The water feels nice and warm.

I bob up and down in the water.
My armbands keep me afloat.

I can put my hands on the bottom.
Soon I will be able to swim.

We hold on to the rail.
I kick my legs as hard as I can.

I let go and paddle with
my hands and kick hard.

8

Now I don't need armbands any more.
We see who can splash the most.

We each have a float to help us.
We hold our floats and kick our legs.

The harder I kick the faster
I can go through the water.

My teacher shows me how to do the crawl.
She tells me how to move my arms and legs.

Sometimes the water gets up my nose
but I don't really mind.

I learn to do the breast stroke too.
I kick my legs like a frog and
push hard with my hands and arms.

I can float on my back.
Soon I will learn back stroke.

Now we are learning to dive.
We all jump into the water together.

16

Next we learn to put our hands above
our heads and dive head first
into the water.
When I'm good at swimming and
diving I want to swim in a race.

These men are in a swimming race.
A good dive gives them a fast start.

18

The first person to touch the bar at
the end of the pool is the winner.

These men are in a back stroke race.
They swim straight down the pool.

These swimmers are making patterns
in the water with their bodies.

Some swimmers even make patterns when they dive under the water.

This girl is diving off a springboard.
She turns a somersault in the air
before she reaches the water.

When you dive like this you must try
to enter the water with your body straight
and your hands in front of you.

When you can swim well there are lots of water sports you can do, like snorkelling. You wear a mask, flippers and a snorkel.

This girl is scuba diving.
She wears a cylinder of air on her back
and breathes through a mask.

Divers can stay under water a long time.
Some divers work on the oil rigs.
Other divers explore wrecks on the sea floor.

Divers built a cradle around this ship,
the *Mary Rose*, so that it could be
lifted from the sea floor.

Lots of people do water sports
in Australia.
Some people like surfing in the big waves
that roll onto the beach.

It takes a lot of practice to
stand up on the surfboard.

Lifeguards watch the people in the water.
They are always ready to rescue someone.

They show people on the beach how to
save lives too.

Index